T0193560

Laila's ABC's of ART

Author:
Alice Bey-Pugh

Illustrated by:
Sameer Kassar

AuthorHouse™
1663 Liberty Drive
Bloomington, IN 47403
www.authorhouse.com
Phone: 833-262-8899

Because of the dynamic nature of the Internet, any web addresses or links contained in this book may have changed since publication and may no longer be valid. The views expressed in this work are solely those of the author and do not necessarily reflect the views of the publisher, and the publisher hereby disclaims any responsibility for them.

This book is printed on acid-free paper.

ISBN: 979-8-8230-1539-4 (sc)
ISBN: 979-8-8230-1538-7 (e)

Library of Congress Control Number: 2023918614

Print information available on the last page.

Published by AuthorHouse 10/09/2023

authorHOUSE®

DEDICATION

To my daughter Laila and all the children who love ART!

A is for Art

Art Gallery

Abstract Painting

Artist

2

B is for Blending

Black   Blue   Brown

Brushes

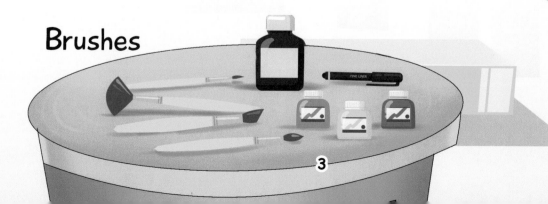

 is for Colors

Contemporary Art

Canvas

Colorful Creations

Charcoal

Chalk

4

 **is for Drawing**

Decorative and Design

Doodle and
Doodling

5

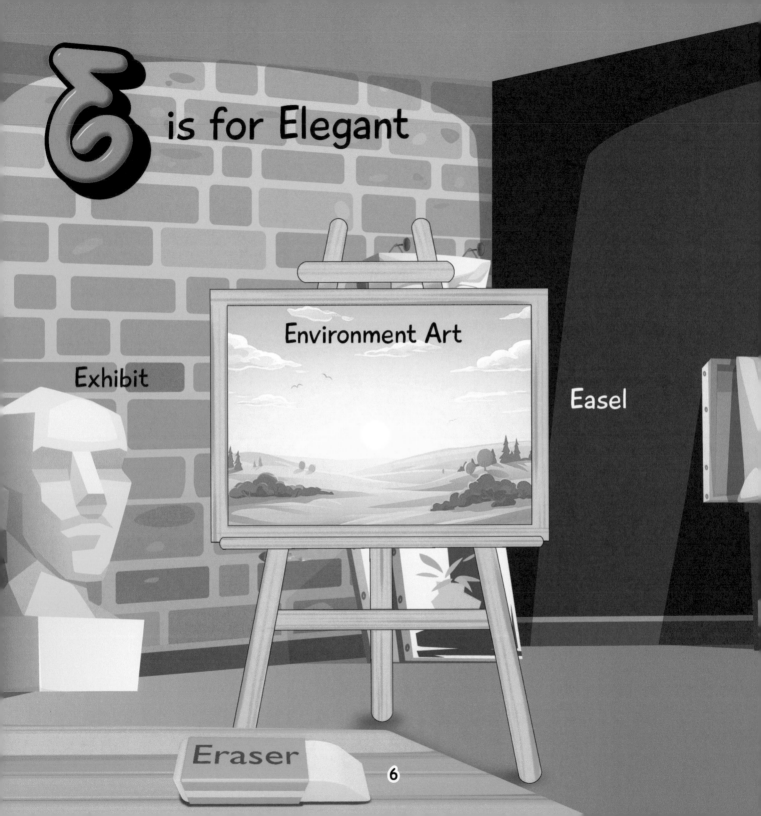

is for Elegant

Exhibit

Environment Art

Easel

Eraser

6

 **is for Frame**

Fresco Art

Fine Art

Funk Art

H is for Harmony

Highlight

Hue

Hieroglyphs

 is for Illustration

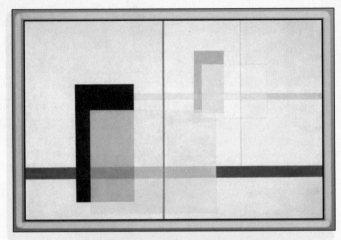

Industrial Design

Imagination Art

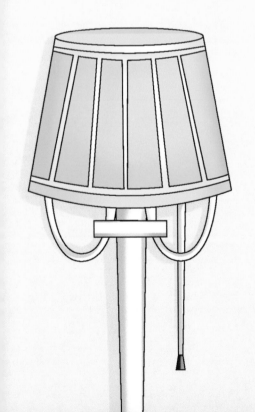

Ink

J is for Jade

Japanese Art

Jade Statue

Juvenile Art

Junk Art

K is for Kinetic

Kinetic Art

Kinetic Pointillism Art

Key Art

Kinesthetic Art

Kitsch Art

Kneaded Eraser

Kirigami Art

12

 is for Logo

Layered Painting

Landscape Painting

Life Painting

13

 **M** is for Masterpiece

Mosaic

Mona Lisa

Muse

Modern Art

Modeling Clay

 is for Neutral

Neon Art

Narrative Art

Natural Color

 **is for Original**

Orange

Oil Painting

Outline

Organic Paint

Origami

16

 **is for Painting**

Pink

Portrait

Pastel

Pencil

Pottery

Paint

Paintbrush

Palette

Purple

17

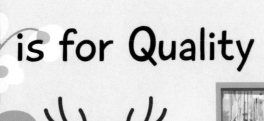

Q is for Quality

Quilt Art

Quattrocento

R is for Red

Renaissance

Realism

S is for Sculpting

Street Art

Sepia Art

Symbolist Art

Sculptor

Sculpture

Stencil Art

Spray Can

Sketchbook

20

T is for Texture

Turquoise Painting

Tempera Painting

Three-Dimensional

Turpentine Painting

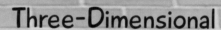

Turpentine Bottle

TURPENTINE BOTTLE

 is for Unique

Umber Art

Ultramarine Art

Urban Art

is for Value

Visual Art

Vintage Artwork

Clear
Varnish

Volume

23

 **is for Watercolor**

Wax Painting

Word Art

Woodblock

Wildlife Art

White Spirit

24

 is for Xylography and
anything exciting

Xylography

25

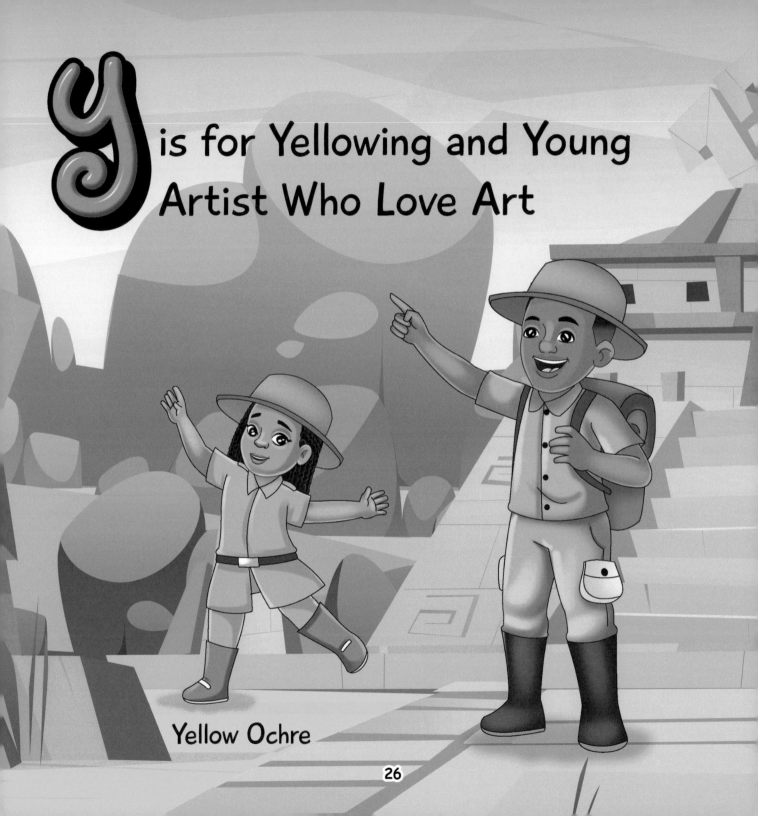

Y is for Yellowing and Young Artist Who Love Art

Yellow Ochre

26

Z is for the Zillion Art Creations One Artist Can Create!

Ziggurat

Zoomorphic

Zenga Art

Zig Zag Sculpture

Z-Pattern Art

The End

Glossary

- **Abstract Painting**: Art where shapes and colors are used to create a feeling or idea, not to look like something specific.

- **Art**: Making beautiful or interesting things with colors, shapes, and imagination.

- **Art Gallery**: A special place where people can go to see and enjoy different artworks.

- **Artist**: Someone who makes art, like paintings, drawings, or sculptures.

- **Black**: A very dark color that's like the night sky with no stars.

- **Blending**: Mixing colors together to make new colors or to create smooth transitions.

- **Blue**: The color of the sky on a clear day.

- **Brown**: The color of tree bark or chocolate.

- **Brushes**: Tools artists use to paint, like a magic wand for colors.

- **Canvas**: A flat, usually white surface where artists paint their pictures.

- **Chalk**: It's a colorful dust stick that can be used for drawing on blackboards and sidewalks.

- **Charcoal**: Artists use this black stick made from compressed burned wood to create smudgy and dark drawings.

- **Colorful Creations**: Beautiful and bright artworks filled with many colors.

- **Colors**: Different shades and hues that make the world pretty and interesting.

- **Contemporary Art**: Art made by artists today, in our modern times.

- **Decorative**: Art that's made to make things look pretty or interesting.

- **Design**: A plan or idea for how something should look or work.

- **Doodle**: Simple drawings made while thinking or daydreaming.

- **Doodling**: Making lots of fun and random drawings.

- **Drawing**: Making pictures with pencils, crayons, or markers.

- **Easel**: A special stand for holding a painting while it's being made.

- **Elegant**: Something that's very fancy and stylish.

- **Environment Art**: Art that shows nature or the world around us.

- **Eraser**: A tool to remove pencil marks and mistakes.

- **Exhibit**: A show where art is displayed for people to see.

- **Fine Art**: Beautiful and special art that's carefully made.

- **Frame**: A border around a picture or painting.

- **Fresco Art**: Painting on wet plaster to create colorful images.

- **Funk Art**: Art that's wild, crazy, and full of surprises.

- **Genre**: Different types or categories of art, like landscapes or portraits.

- **Glitter**: Sparkly stuff that shines and adds magic to art.

- **Graffiti**: Colorful writing or pictures on walls or surfaces.

- **Green**: The color of grass and leaves.

- **Grey**: A color that's not quite black or white, like rainy skies.

- **Harmony**: When colors and shapes go together and look nice.

- **Hieroglyphs**: Ancient symbols or drawings used in writing.

- **Highlight**: Making something stand out by adding brightness or color.

- **Hue**: Another word for color, like red, blue, or green.

- **Illustration**: Pictures that help tell a story in books or magazines.

- **Imagination Art**: Art that comes from your creative ideas and dreams.

- **Industrial Design**: Creating useful things that look cool and work well.

- **Ink**: Liquid that's used for drawing and writing.

- **Jade**: A beautiful green stone that's sometimes used in art.

- **Jade Statue**: A sculpture made of jade, a precious stone.

- **Japanese Art**: Art made by people from Japan, known for its beauty and culture.

- **Junk Art**: Art made from old or discarded things, like a treasure hunt.

- **Juvenile Art**: Art made by kids and young artists.

- **Key Art**: Pictures or images that represent the main characters or themes of a movie, video game, or story, often used for posters or covers.

- **Kinesthetic Art**: Art that moves or changes when touched.

- **Kinetic**: Art that moves or has motion, like a dancing sculpture.

- **Kinetic Art**: Art that moves or changes, like a spinning mobile.

- **Kinetic Pointillism Art**: Art made with tiny dots that seem to move.

- **Kirigami Art**: Paper art where you fold and cut to create amazing designs.

- **Kitsch Art**: Art that's intentionally funny or weird.

- **Kneaded Eraser**: A soft and squishy eraser that artists use to gently remove pencil marks and create special effects in their drawings.

- **Landscape Painting**: Art that shows beautiful outdoor scenes.

- **Layered Painting**: Art with different parts stacked on top of each other.

- **Life Painting**: Painting real people or things as they look in real life.

- **Logo**: A special design or symbol that represents something.

- **Masterpiece**: A really amazing and perfect piece of art.

- **Modeling Clay**: Soft and moldable clay that artists use to create 3D sculptures and shapes, like making animals, people, or objects with their hands.

- **Modern Art**: Art that's new and different from traditional styles.

- **Mona Lisa**: A famous painting of a mysterious woman by Leonardo da Vinci.

- **Mosaic**: Art made by arranging small colored pieces into a pattern.

- **Muse**: Something that inspires an artist to create.

- **Natural Color**: Colors that we see in nature, like the red, orange, and brown leaves of Fall.

- **Narrative Art**: Art that tells a story or shows a sequence of events.

- **Neon Art**: Bright, glowing art that uses neon lights.

- **Neutral**: Colors that are calm and don't stand out, like beige.

- **Oil Painting**: Painting with colors mixed in oil, known for its rich colors.

- **Orange**: A bright color like fruit, a mix of red and yellow.

- **Organic Paint**: Paint made from natural things like plants.

- **Origami**: Folding paper to make cool shapes and animals.

- **Original**: Art that's one-of-a-kind and not a copy.

- **Outline**: The outer shape of an object or drawing.

- **Paint**: Liquid colors used to create pictures.

- **Paintbrush**: A tool with bristles used to apply paint.

- **Painting**: Creating images with paint on a canvas or paper.

- **Palette**: A flat board to mix and hold paint colors.

- **Pastel**: Soft and light colors like those in a sunset.

- **Pencil**: A tool for drawing or writing with a thin, pointed tip.

- **Pink**: A pretty and light shade of red.

- **Portrait**: A painting or drawing of a person's face.

- **Pottery**: Art made by shaping and firing clay into useful objects.

- **Purple**: A rich color that's a mix of red and blue.

- **Quality**: How good something is, like a high-quality artwork.

- **Quattrocento**: An Italian word that means "fifteenth century" and refers to the art and culture of the 15th century in Italy.

- **Quilt Art**: Creating art by sewing pieces of fabric together.

- **Realism**: Art that looks like it's from the real world.

- **Red**: A bright and warm color, like fire.

- **Renaissance**: Artworks created during the Renaissance period, known for their realistic and lifelike qualities, often featuring religious and mythological themes.

- **Sculpture**: Making art by shaping materials like clay, stone, or metal into 3D shapes or statues.

- **Sculptor**: Someone who makes sculptures, like statues or 3D art.

- **Sculpting**: The act of shaping materials to create sculptures.

- **Sepia Art**: Art in shades of brown, like old photographs.

- **Sketchbook**: A special book for drawing and doodling.

- **Spray Can**: A can that sprays paint, often used in street art.

- **Stencil Art**: Using a template to spray or paint the same design multiple times.

- **Street Art**: Art created outdoors on streets, walls, or public places, often colorful and creative.

- **Symbolist Art**: Art that uses symbols and images to represent ideas or feelings.

- **Tempera Painting**: A type of paint that uses egg yolks to mix colors.

- **Texture**: How something feels when you touch it, like smooth, rough, or bumpy.

- **Three-Dimensional**: Art that has height, width, and depth, like sculptures you can touch.

- **Turpentine Bottle**: A container that holds the liquid turpentine used in painting.

- **Turpentine Painting**: Art created using a liquid called turpentine to thin or clean paint.

- **Turquoise Painting**: Artwork that uses the color turquoise, which is a pretty blue-green.

- **Ultramarine Art**: Art that features a deep blue color called ultramarine.

- **Umber Art**: Art that uses a brown color called umber.

- **Unique**: One-of-a-kind and different from everything else.

- **Urban Art**: Art created in cities, often found on walls and streets.

- **Value**: How light or dark something is in a painting or drawing.

- **Vintage Artwork**: Art that's old and from a different time, like a treasure from the past.

- **Visual Art**: Art that you can see, like paintings, sculptures, and drawings.

- **Volume**: How much space something takes up, like a big sculpture.

- **Watercolor**: A painting with special, watery paints that create soft and flowing colors on paper.

- **Wax Painting**: Art made using wax, like crayons or melted wax.

- **White Spirit**: A clear liquid that artists sometimes use to clean paint from brushes and surfaces.

- **Wildlife Art**: Art that features animals and nature.

- **Word Art**: Art that's made with words and letters, like a cool design with words.

- **Woodblock**: A piece of wood with a design carved into it for printing.

- **Xylography**: A fancy word for woodblock printing, where images are printed from wood.

- **Yellowing**: When something turns yellow with age, like old paper.

- **Yellow Ochre**: A yellow-brown color often used in art.

- **Zenga Art:** Special paintings from Japan that tell stories using both pictures and fancy writing, like art with a hidden message.

- **Z-Pattern Art**: Art with lines and shapes that make a "Z" shape.

- **Zig-Zag Sculpture**: A sculpture with a pattern that goes up and down like a zigzag.

- **Ziggurat**: A type of ancient pyramid-shaped building.

- **Zillion**: A super big number, like having lots and lots of something.

- **Zoomorphic**: Art that looks like animals or is inspired by them.

Printed in the United States
by Baker & Taylor Publisher Services